Hunting for the Northern Lights

Written by
Cath Jones

Illustrated by
Sara Gibbeson

Philippa Smith was fed up.

"I have waited all my life to see the northern lights," she said. "But whenever we travel, we stay close to home. You can't see the lights near us, so I never get to see them."

Mr Smith was Philippa's dad. He was not so keen to see the northern lights.

"It's just a display of lights at night," he said. "It's **so** boring!"

Philippa still wished to see the lights. So she and her mum booked tickets for some flights.

"The whole of this trip will be a hunt for the northern lights," she said to her mum.

"Which flights did you book?" asked Mrs Smith.

"Lots!" said Philippa. "I booked tickets for flights to Alaska, Scotland, Finland and Norway. It will be fun!"

On Monday they flew to Alaska.

"The northern lights are common in Alaska. I think we will see them," said Philippa.

They did! They saw white and greenish lights glittering in the night air.

"Wow! Stunning!" whispered Mr Smith. "You are right, Philippa. They aren't boring at all!"

On Wednesday, they flew to Finland.

When it got dark, they went dog sledding. It was a splendid way to see the northern lights.

The lights flickered like flames.

Mr and Mrs Smith enjoyed the lights just as much as Philippa.

On Friday, they went to Svalbard in Norway. It was a long way from the big towns.

"It needs to be dark and clear to see the northern lights," said Philippa.

But there were lots of clouds.

That night, the north wind blew the clouds out of the way.

The three Smiths lay in their tent and looked up.

The northern lights looked like soft velvet, twisting and twirling in the air.

"Dazzling!" whispered Mr Smith.

The next night, they went out in a big boat in the dark.

"The lights look just like stars," whispered Mr Smith.

On Tuesday night, they lay on the ground, looking up. A streak of bright red and green lights lit up their tent.

On Thursday, they trekked into the wilderness on foot.

The northern lights were fantastic. They grew bigger and bigger, with lots of shimmering green and pink lights.

On Saturday, they flew to Scotland. They saw the northern lights from the plane!

On Sunday, they flew back home.

When they got home, Mr Smith thanked Philippa.

"I am so glad we saw the northern lights," he said. "They weren't boring at all. Let's go back soon!"